On the Minting of Money

500th Anniversary Edition

1526 – 2026

MORE FROM THE WEBSTERS' PRESS

The Websters' Dictionary

Redefining the Future of the Economy

Blockchain with American Character

The Capitalist Manifesto

The Ten Commandments of Capitalism

The 21st Century Gold Standard

websterspress.com

On the Minting of Money

by Nicolaus Copernicus (1526)

Translated from the original Latin by Gerald Malsbary

Edited by Ralph Benko

Second Edition

THE WEBSTERS' PRESS

Washington D.C.

Cover Art: *Astronomer Copernicus, or Conversations with God* by Jan Matejko (1838-1893) from Jagiellonian University Museum in Krakow, Poland.

ISBN: 978-0-9820756-2-3

This book is dedicated to a Bishop of Rome who Nicolaus Copernicus would have greatly admired.

His Holiness Pope Leo XIV

APPRECIATION

Profound gratitude is due to the co-editor of the first edition, Charles Kadlec, without whom this second version would not exist. Likewise to the technical editor of this edition, Andy Fluke, for his assistance with this update for the 500th anniversary of the text.

CONTENTS

FOREWORD TO THE 2013 EDITION

by Lewis E. Lehrman

A Great Scientist and His Money

WE ABIDE IN A SOLAR SYSTEM first revealed by the great astronomer Nicolaus Copernicus. So it was that the equally great astronomer Ptolemy, one millennium and a half after his death, did yield to the genius of his peer, Copernicus. The mathematical proofs that Ptolemy used to show the Earth as the center of the solar system were superseded by the verifiable calculations of Copernicus. The Earth did revolve regularly around the sun, not the other way 'round as Ptolemy's detailed calculations suggested.

Thus, we live in a Copernican world, preceded by the "Copernican revolution."

To read and reread the treatise of Copernicus on the minting of money is to see a true genius at work establishing the scientific rules of the monetary universe — that is, the earthly monetary economy that carried the world beyond barter and into the realm of economic growth and the industrial revolution.

What Copernicus established as the scientific rules governing money are as true today as are the path-breaking rules of Copernicus governing the solar system.

Read on and see for yourself.

Lewis E. Lehrman

June 2013

FOREWORD TO THE 2026 EDITION

by Kurt Schuler

A Monetary Standard

NICOLAUS COPERNICUS (1473-1543) was as astute an observer of the Earth as of the heavens. His theory placing the Sun rather than the Earth at the center of the universe, published shortly before his death, revolutionized astronomy and humanity's view of its place in the cosmos. His pithy essay on money, unfortunately, was not published until 300 years after he wrote it. Though it is now 500 years old, it remains worth the short time necessary to read it.

The surface subject of the essay is coins, which no longer have the centrality in trade that they did in Copernicus's time. The deeper topic, though, is the monetary standard, which remains one of the most important issues in economics. Copernicus packed into a short space several important ideas that many much longer writings on money have neglected. To wit:

* The debasement of coinage, or as we would now say, inflation, is subtle but highly damaging.
* Money's value as money may differ from its value as metal.

* Money worth more as metal than as currency disappears from circulation to be melted down — a version of Gresham's Law that "bad money drives out good" when governments try to force people to accept both at the same rate.
* The long-term tendency of governments is to depreciate the currency.
* Depreciation of the currency drives prices up — a version of the Quantity Theory of Money.
* Depreciation creates some short-term monetary gain for the ruler, who creates the currency, but is typically harmful for the populace.
* A uniform and universal currency, if it can be a good one, is the most desirable. (Copernicus focuses on the immediate problems of coinage in the part of Europe he lived in, but the principle is clearly capable of extension.)

Copernicus's observation that inflation is "noticed only by a few very thoughtful people" is a forerunner of John Maynard Keynes's famous remark centuries later, in his book The Economic Consequences of the Peace (1919), that "Lenin is said to have declared that the best way to destroy the Capitalist System was to debauch the currency. By a continuing process of inflation, governments can confiscate, secretly and unobserved, an important part of the wealth of their citizens. … The process engages all the hidden forces of economic law on the side of destruction, and does it in a manner which not one man in a million is able to diagnose."

Nowadays, inflation has been going on for so long that ordinary citizens do notice it. The surprising thing is that we have become so used to it that most people don't stop to ask themselves if a better system exists. Consider, though, that under the Bretton Woods version of the gold standard (1946-1971), the U.S. dollar was pegged to gold at $35 per troy ounce. Currently it is $4,500 per ounce. The U.S. consumer price index has risen less dramatically, but is still at eight times its level just before the United States abandoned the gold standard. And the United States has had one of the world's best-performing monetary policies during that time. The monetary standard really matters!

Kurt Schuler

Senior Fellow in Financial History
Center for Financial Stability, New York
September 2025

INTRODUCTION

by Ralph Benko

The Golden Intellectual Provenance of the Gold Standard

THE CLASSICAL GOLD STANDARD has a more profound pedigree than many know.

It is fairly widely understood that the classical gold standard originally was designed, in 1717, by Sir Isaac Newton, then master of the mint of Great Britain. It lasted for two centuries, and it is an irony of history that John Law's notorious experiment with paper money, which ruined his investors, France, and himself and lasted but three years, was initiated in the same year.

The fact of Newton's role as architect alone would provide the gold standard with a most dignified intellectual provenance. Now comes a new, meticulously researched, and lucidly devised translation by classicist Gerald Malsbary (PhD, University of Toronto, 1988; currently director of first-year symposium at Belmont Abbey College).

Through this translation, scholars, intellectuals, and policy makers readily will be able to discern that the fundamental intellectual groundwork for the classical gold standard was laid by another scientific icon, Nicolaus Copernicus. Yes, Copernicus, the very same who placed the sun in the center of the solar system.

Prof. Malsbary's translation shows Copernicus's widely overlooked tract *On the Minting of Money* as no more dated than heliocentricity, contemporary and as lucid as anything ever written on monetary policy. Copernicus was as great a stylist as Lord Keynes. And, as his fundamental breakthrough in astronomy suggests, Copernicus was the more rigorously scientific thinker.

Copernicus's observations are as pertinent today as when he composed them in 1526. Prof. Malsbary has compared all available extant earlier translations of this work into English and, moreover, provides a rich critical apparatus. Malsbary hereby furnishes an invaluable addition both to scholarship and to the contemporary policy discourse, now fomenting in the United States Congress and around the world, on monetary reform.

Economists seek to present their work as rigorous science. It therefore is an irony and an oddity that modern academic economists find themselves falling within the political provenance of William Jennings Bryan and Richard Nixon rather than the scientific provenance of Copernicus and Newton.

Bryan's great silver-tongued speech at the Democratic convention of 1896 propelled him then, and twice later, to a presidential nomination and finally into the role of secretary of state under President Wilson. On the convention floor he declaimed against the restoration of the classical gold standard. "You shall not press down upon the brow of labor this crown of thorns. You shall not crucify mankind upon a cross of gold."

And yet, notwithstanding these resounding phrases (which failed to propel him into the presidency, which went to his Republican rival, William McKinley, who instituted the gold standard in 1900), Bryan was not greatly respected by his contemporaries as a thinker. As Roger T. Johnson wrote in Historical Beginnings … The Federal Reserve (published by the Federal Reserve Bank of Boston, revised 2010, p. 20).

> For years Bryan had a reputation as one of the nation's most outstanding and enthralling public speakers, but some people who knew him best believed that the power of his oratory concealed the paucity of his intellect. One of his cabinet colleagues later sneered: "I discovered that one could drive a prairie schooner through any part of his argument and never scrape against a fact or a sound statement."

More ironically yet, Bryan today probably is best remembered for his role in prosecuting Tennessee schoolteacher John Scopes for daring to teach evolution in the public schools of Tennessee — as dramatized in the play Inherit the Wind. How odd, then, that the academic experts should ignore Copernicus and Newton to embrace the position of Bryan, a creationist, in championing fiduciary paper currency (itself monetary creationism).

How odd, also, that academics, almost unanimously of a progressive political bent, should find themselves apologists for a monetary policy visited upon the world by Richard Nixon. Nixon was, from his earliest days, and remains in memory, something of a *bête noire* of progressives. And yet the preeminent progressive economists of today find themselves in effect apologists for a policy the legacy of Richard M. Nixon.

Even Karl Marx was for the gold standard. And yet, progressives remain the only remaining enthusiastic champions of the last vestige of Nixon's "New Economic Policy," the final repudiation of the gold standard. It strikes this writer as no coincidence that the stagnation of middle-class earnings — and the emergence of severe income inequality — correlates tightly with the embrace of a system of free-floating (or, rather, sinking) paper currency.

Why, then, do progressive academic economists obsessively defend this last artifact of Nixonomics? A vast, and unwarranted, disdain among economists clouds the reputation of the classical gold standard. The most likely answer derives from what the late professor Jacques Rueff (member of L'Académie française and of the Ordre national de la Légion d'honneur), writing in *The Monetary Sin of the West* (Macmillan Company, 1972, pp. 23–24), termed "the outcome of an unbelievable collective mistake which, when people become aware of it, will be viewed by history as an object of astonishment and scandal."

The "unbelievable collective mistake" that he refers to was the supplanting of the classical, or true, gold standard with the "gold-exchange standard." The Great Depression was attributed, falsely (although not maliciously), to the gold standard. But the true gold standard had been suspended almost a decade prior, at Genoa, to be replaced by its "evil twin," the superficially similar but inherently defective gold-exchange standard. Prof. Rueff called it a grotesque caricature of the gold standard.

Public intellectuals (although not, yet, most academic economists) are beginning to unwind this crucial collapsed distinction. Perforce, new interest in the classical gold standard is beginning to arise in the policy discourse. A renewed appreciation of the classical gold standard is evident from the fact of its proponents recently being treated with dignity in respected venues such as ProCon.org, Debate.org, and IntelligenceSquared.com.

Perhaps Hayek (himself no proponent of the classical gold standard), in his Nobel Prize lecture delivered December 11, 1974, put his finger on the root cause of the disdain that academic economists show toward the classical gold standard. He entitled this lecture "The Pretence of Knowledge":

> "There is as much reason to be apprehensive about the long run dangers created in a much wider field by the uncritical acceptance of assertions which have the *appearance* of being scientific as there is with regard to the problems I have just discussed. What I mainly wanted to bring out by the topical illustration is that certainly in my field, but I believe also generally in the sciences of man, what looks superficially like the most scientific procedure is often the most unscientific, and, beyond this, that in these fields there are definite limits to what we can expect science to achieve. This means that to entrust to science — or to deliberate control according to scientific principles — more than scientific method can achieve may have deplorable effects.

The progress of the natural sciences in modern times has of course so much exceeded all expectations that any suggestion that there may be some limits to it is bound to arouse suspicion. Especially all those will resist such an insight who have hoped that our increasing power of prediction and control, generally regarded as the characteristic result of scientific advance, applied to the processes of society, would soon enable us to mould society entirely to our liking. It is indeed true that, in contrast to the exhilaration which the discoveries of the physical sciences tend to produce, the insights which we gain from the study of society more often have a dampening effect on our aspirations; and it is perhaps not surprising that the more impetuous younger members of our profession are not always prepared to accept this. Yet the confidence in the unlimited power of science is only too often based on a false belief that the scientific method consists in the application of a readymade technique, or in imitating the form rather than the substance of scientific procedure, as if one needed only to follow some cooking recipes to solve all social problems. It sometimes almost seems as if the techniques of science were more easily learnt than the thinking that shows us what the problems are and how to approach them.... If we are to safeguard the reputation of science, and to prevent the arrogation of knowledge based on a superficial similarity of procedure with that of the physical sciences, much effort will have to be directed toward debunking such arrogations, some of which have by now become the vested

interests of established university departments."
(Emphasis in original.)

Consider, though, that from 1792 the United States, under Treasury Secretary Alexander Hamilton, putting the US on a bimetallic gold and silver standard, the conversion price of the dollar to gold was $20.67/oz. The interwar gold standard, adopted at Genoa in 1922 replaced the gold standard with the gold-exchange standard.

The gold-exchange standard was characterized by French economist Jacques Rueff as "a grotesque caricature" of the gold standard, having the superficial appearance of a gold standard without the mechanisms to effect world monetary stability. This devolution is comprehensively outlined by Prof. Robert Mundell in his 1999 Nobel Prize in Economics acceptance speech.

That substitution of the gold-exchange standard for the classical gold standard caused (as noted by agricultural economist George Warren — the leading commodity price expert of his era and FDR's original monetary policy advisor) an increase in the general price level by 50%. The price of gold was fixed to its pre-war parity.

This contributed to — in the opinion of Rueff, caused — the Great Depression.

Warren, recognizing the toxic deflationary pressure caused thereby, persuaded FDR to revalue the dollar to $35/oz. As documented by Liaquat Ahamed in his Pulitzer Prize in History-winning *Lords of Finance: The Bankers Who Broke the World*, this revaluation promptly lifted the Great Depression ... until the Treasury, unclear on the concept, sterilized the resulting international gold inflows to the US. A severe second dip ensued.

From 1934 to 1971, the U.S. dollar was legally defined at $35 per troy ounce of gold. This was internationally codified from 1946 to 1971 under the Bretton Woods international monetary system.

Thereby, most other currencies were legally convertible to the gold-convertible dollar, making the dollar the world's reserve currency, a status characterized by French finance minister (later president) Valery Giscard d'Estaing as an "exorbitant privilege."

President Lyndon Johnson, *de facto*, and President Richard Nixon, *de jure* (in "temporarily closing the gold window" on the deeply unfortunate advice of his Treasury Secretary John Connally) brought an end to the last remnants of the gold standard. Their unmooring of the dollar has caused a sustained loss of value, with gold, as of this writing, trading over $4,500 per ounce.

Presumably, Copernicus and young Keynes would have been horrified. But not surprised.

The more impetuous members of the profession of economics, whether young or old, indeed could benefit by soberly "debunking such arrogations." To begin this there hardly can be a better place to start than Copernicus's *On the Minting of Money*.

Profound gratitude is due to this volume's co-editor, Charles Kadlec, for the critical role he played in commissioning Prof. Malsbary to undertake this project. Frs. Vincent Fitzpatrick and C. John McCloskey deserve recognition and appreciation for their providential roles in finding and effecting an introduction to Prof. Malsbary. Likewise to the technical editor of the 2026 edition, Andy Fluke, for his assistance with this update for the 500th anniversary of the text.

Special heartfelt thanks are offered to Lewis E. Lehrman, the great living disciple of Prof. Rueff and eminence grise of the classical gold standard and author of, among other significant works, *The True Gold Standard* and *Money, Gold, and History*, for furnishing the foreword to Prof. Malsbary's new translation of this timeless classic.

In addition to the gratitude to those already referenced herein, in justice let tribute be paid to the valiant ones who kept raised the torch beside the golden door during the classical gold standard's long eclipse. The roster, too long to recite in its entirety, includes the Hon. Jack Kemp, George Gilder, Dr. Arthur B. Laffer, the Hon. S.S. Tarapore, the Hon. Manuel Hinds, Sean Fieler, Paul Fabra, Prof. Brian Domitrovich, Prof. William Luther, Prof. Lawrence White, Prof. Richard Timberlake, Prof. Steve Hanke, Dr. Ron Paul, Dr. Kurt Schuler, Dr. Lawrence Parks, Steve Forbes, Lydia Mashburn Newman, Doug Centilli, John Allison, John Tamny, James Grant, Howard Segermark, Seth Lipsky, Richard Lowrie, Hugo Salinas-Price, John Mueller, Nathan Lewis, and members of the rising generation such as Rich Danker and Jonathan Decker. The world remains much indebted to the great Jacques Rueff.

It is an honor to present *On the Minting of Money*, by Nicolaus Copernicus (1526), translated from the original Latin by Gerald Malsbary with his prefatory remarks and bibliography. The elegance of the provenance of the gold standard hereby is restored to its deserved level.

Ralph Benko
January 2026

On the Minting of Money

A new translation of Nicolaus Copernicus's

Monetae Cudendae Ratio

by Gerald Malsbary

TRANSLATOR'S PREFACE

by Gerald Malsbary

Prefatory Remarks and Bibliography

NICOLAUS COPERNICUS the astronomer embodies the modern scientific ideal: the revolutionary revealer of a new, verifiable scientific theory that shocks our conventional perceptions. However, it is not very widely known, outside of Eastern Europe at least, that Copernicus also spent about twenty years working on economic theory. His treatise *On the Minting of Money* (*Monetae Cudendae Ratio*), was first printed in 1826, three hundred years after its composition in 1525–1526. At the time, the semi-autonomous ecclesiastical region between Poland and Prussia where he lived (Varmia) was undergoing a political and economic metamorphosis, and his judgment and expertise (a fruit of the best late Scholastic and Humanist learning) was summoned by the Prussian and Polish governments to help stabilize an inflated currency. Was his insight into monetary matters as revolutionary as his astronomy?

Copernicus repeatedly emphasizes the difference between the "value" in precious metal (*valor*) and the "valuation" (*aestimatio*). In order for money to be good, it must not only have a reliable, and not constantly decreasing, precious metal content; it must also have value qua money: the sign stamped on the coin, implying trust in the political authority, also adds a small, but important, value. Recent researches into the origin of money in early Greek civilization have pointed out that the synthesis of intrinsic value and conventional value was a crucial step towards modern money. Can Copernicus's insights — which have not yet become a part of mainstream economic theory — help clarify in some way the original reason for money in Western civilization? Another recurring theme is his dislike of government making a profit from the minting of money through the use of less and less silver — the provision of reliable, good money, he maintains, should be a "nonprofit" service on the part of the government to the wellbeing of the people. Does this approach involve a "moral" approach to monetary policy?

The answers to such questions must be left to students of economics and philosophy, who will be able to place Copernicus's conclusions in a larger context. Meanwhile, it has been my task here simply to provide another updated English translation of the Latin original, in order to bring back to light, or at least a little more into the foreground, an important primary source in the history of economic thought that appears to have been unduly neglected by economics students today, especially in the light of the author's immense scientific reputation. The treatise has been translated into Polish, Italian, French, German, and English, and there have been to date at least four in English published since 1955 (1955, 1965, 1979, and 1985). Unfortunately, these translations are rather hard to access since they were privately printed or have appeared only as journal articles. Edward Rosen's most recent, critically annotated English translation and commentary (in the Polish Academy of Sciences edition), while very full of helpful learning, is somewhat inconvenient in its format and does not include the Latin text. The most helpful work of scholarship I have found has been in German: Erich Sommerfeld's 1978 critical edition of Copernicus's essay, together with related contemporary texts, and accompanied by a commentary. Further reading in the literature listed below will also reveal that the Polish and Prussian governments of the time did not take his advice and continued to follow a program of debasing the currency.

According to Erich Sommerfeld, one of Copernicus's most important contributions was his creation of a monetary theory based on his own empirical observation and archival research, and free of any explicitly theological or Aristotelian formulae. Copernicus's study of the monetary situation began as early as 1504, soon after his return to his native country from studies in Cracovia and Northern Italy. His first version of the treatise was written in 1517, his third and last version in 1526. He presented his ideas both orally and in writing on several occasions before the West Prussian estates. Copernicus's concern to communicate to a wide and practical-minded audience is clear both from the epilogue and from the fact that one version was composed in early German.

The division into three sections ("Theoretical Foundations," "The Debasement of Prussian Currency: A Brief History," and "A Plan for Reform") is taken from Sommerfeld's edition.

Bibliography

Copernicus, Nicolaus. *Treatise on Coining Money.* Translated and edited by George A. Moore. Chevy Chase, MD: Country Dollar Press, 1965[1526].

Reiss, Timothy J. and Roger H. Hinderliter. "Money and Value in the Sixteenth Century: the *Monetae Cudendae Ratio* of Nicholas Copernicus." *Journal of the History of Ideas* 40 (1979): 293–313.

Rosen, Edward. *Minor Works.* Vol. 3 of *Nicholas Copernicus Complete Works.* Baltimore, MD: Johns Hopkins University Press, 1992[1985], 167–215.

Seaford, Richard. *Money and the Early Greek Mind: Homer, Philosophy, Tragedy.* Cambridge: Cambridge University Press, 2004.

Sommerfeld, Erich. *Die Geldlehre des Nicolaus Copernicus: Texte, Übersetzungen, Kommentare.* Vaduz, Liechtenstein: Topos Verlag, 1978.

Taylor, J. "Copernicus on the Evils of Inflation and the Establishment of a Sound Currency." *Journal of History of Ideas* 16 (1955): 540–547.

Volckart, Oliver. "Early beginnings of the quantity theory of money and their context in Polish and Prussian monetary policies, c. 1520–1550." *Economic History Review* 50 (1997):3, 430–449.

Monetae Cudendae Ratio

1526

ON THE MINTING OF MONEY

Nicolaus Copernicus

Theoretical Foundations

ALTHOUGH THERE ARE COUNTLESS MALADIES that are forever causing the decline of kingdoms, princedoms, and republics, the following four (in my judgment) are the most serious: civil discord, a high death rate, sterility of the soil, and the debasement of coinage. The first three are so obvious that everybody recognizes the damage they cause; but the fourth one, which has to do with money, is noticed by only a few very thoughtful people, since it does not operate all at once and at a single blow, but gradually overthrows governments, and in a hidden, insidious way.

Money, or coinage, is gold or silver that has been specially marked — in accordance with policy established by any government or head of government — for the purpose of reckoning the prices of things that are bought and sold. Money is therefore a kind of common "measuring stick" for the valuation of things. Now, whatever is taken as a measure has to be stable — must keep to a fixed limit. Otherwise, public order will necessarily be disturbed, and the buyers and sellers of things will be cheated many times over, just as if basic measures of length [Latin *ulna*, or *ell*], bulk measure

[Latin *modius*, or *peck*], or weight did not have a fixed quantity. Now, I think that the relevant measure here is the *valuation* [Latin *aestimatio*] of the money as such, and, although this is *founded* in the quality of the metal it is made of, nevertheless, money's material or metallic value [Latin *valor*] must be distinguished from its valuation as money [*aestimatio*]; for money can be valued more in itself than the material it is composed of and vice versa [i.e., its material value may be more than its actual valuation].[1]

It is necessary for money to be established: even though exchange could also take place simply by weights of gold or silver alone (since, by universal human consent, gold and silver are everywhere highly valued); nevertheless, money is needed for two reasons: first, because of the inconvenience of always having to carry around heavy weights of metal, and second, because the real value of the metals is not easily grasped by everyone at a glance. Thus it has become customary to mark money with a public seal, by means of which the proper amount of gold or silver is indicated as present in each coin, and that the public authority is to be trusted in this.

It is customary for coins — especially silver coins — to be made with an alloy of bronze,[2] and this for two reasons (as I judge at least): (1) that the coins be less exposed to the danger of being hoarded up and remelted than they would be if they were made of pure silver and (2) so that the silver divided up into tiny portions, by being mixed with bronze, can have a convenient size in the form of small coins; a third reason can be added as well: (3) with the support of the bronze alloy, the coins will last longer and not quickly wear away with use.

Now a correct and fair valuation of money is in place when each coin holds slightly less gold or silver than the amount of gold or silver it can buy: the difference would be the added value due to the expense of minting the coins. The mark put on the coin, that is to say, must add some worth to the material as such.[3]

This worth is cheapened, for the most part, through too much quantity [of silver]: that is to say, if so much silver is made into coins that people desire the sheer mass of the silver[4] more than the money itself; in this way, the worth of the money [*dignitas*] is damaged when it is not possible to buy as much silver by its means as the money itself contains, and a greater value is realized by destroying (i.e., melting down) the money to get the silver. The remedy for this problem is to withhold from the coining of new money until it equals out, and the money is worth more than the silver.[5]

The [material] value of money is lessened in many ways: either through defect of material alone, namely, when more bronze is mixed with silver than is right for that particular weight of coin; or through the loss of [total] weight of the coin, even though the proportion of bronze to silver is correct; or (and this is the worst case) through both of these defects occurring at the same time; finally, the value can just diminish on its own through usage, over a long passage of time, and this is the only reason for making new money. The evidence of this happening is, if the silver in the money is found to be significantly less than what can be bought with it — and this is rightly considered debasement [or *poverty*: Latin *penuria*] of the currency.[6]

The Debasement of Prussian Currency, A Brief History

THESE BASIC PRINCIPLES of coinage having been set out, let us consider the specific case of Prussian monetary history, and show, first, how it reached such a low level of value.

This money circulates under the names of *marks*, *scots*, and so forth, and there are also weights going by the same names: a *weighed* mark [i.e., a mark "of weight" — Latin *marcha ponderis*] is one half-pound. But a *counted* mark [i.e., a mark *of money* — Latin *marcha numeri*] consists of sixty *solids* [Latin *solidi*, French *sous*, German *schillings*]. All this is commonly known. In order to ward off any confusion about these two kinds of mark, from this point forward, whenever the term *mark* is used, it will be understood to refer to the *counted* or money type of mark; by the name of *pound* [Latin *libra*], however, a weight of two [*weighed*] marks will be signified, it being understood that a half-pound is equivalent to one mark of weight.

Now, we learn from ancient archives and written accounts that, under the reign of Conrad of Jungingen,[7] (i.e., not long before the Battle of Tannenberg[8] [1410]), a ½-pound (or 1 mark) of pure silver could be purchased for 2 Prussian marks [of money] and 8 scots,[9] when a 1/4th part of bronze was alloyed with 3/4ths of silver. From a ½-pound of that [alloyed] mass they made 112 *solidi* [or *schillings*].[10] Adding 1/3rd of this to it (1/3rd of 112 equals 37 1/3) makes a total of 149, plus 2 *denarii* [i.e. 2 *obols* or pennies, each a 1/6th part of a schilling: or 1/3rd of a schilling] making 149 1/3 schillings, weighing 2/3rd of a whole pound, or

32 scots of silver [i.e., 24 for a 1-weight mark plus 8 for another 1/3rd of a mark], which will clearly be 3/4th pure silver (and that was a ½-pound of pure silver to begin with [in weight]). But it has already been said that the price of that much silver was 140 *solidi* per ½-pound. The other 9 1/3 solids were accounted for by the value of the coinage per se [i.e., its *aestimatio*].[11] In this way its valuation was conveniently correlated with its material value.

This was the money of Winrich [of Kniprode], and Conrad and Ulrich [of Jungingen],[12] and pieces of it can still be found in their treasuries. But after the defeat of Prussia and the battle mentioned above, the decline of the republic began to appear in the currency. The *solids* [i.e., *schillings*] under Heinrich,[13] although they looked just like the ones we described above, have been discovered to contain no more than 3/5ths silver. This error progressed to the point where there were 3 parts of bronze to a 1/4th part of silver — the exact inverse of before. It was really "copper money," not silver anymore, even though the weight was still 112 solids per ½-pound.[14] But since it does not at all make sense to introduce new, good money while the old, cheaper money is still in circulation, so much the more was it mistaken to introduce new, cheaper money when the old, better money was still circulating, because this not only tainted the old money, but as it were, overthrew it completely. The administration of Michael [of Sternberg] and [Paul Belitzer of] Rusdorff[15] wanted to fix this problem and bring the currency back to its original state. They minted new *solidi* that we now call *grossi*; but since it didn't seem possible to abolish the older, cheaper money without taking a substantial loss, the old solidi remained in use along with the new, and this was a signal error.

Two "old schillings" now passed for one of the new, and now the people had a double kind of mark, made of old schillings or of new ones. The new or good mark, and the old or cheap mark, were both worth sixty schillings. *Obols* [smallest unit, a kind of *penny*] remained in use, but for an old schilling six were exchanged, for a new one, twelve. (We can easily gather from this that originally a *solidus* was made up of twelve *obols*. For just as we call a fifteenth part a *mandel*, so in many parts of Germany the word *schilling* is used for a twelfth part). But the name of *novi solidi* [or *new schillings*] remained until the times when I can remember: how they eventually became *grossi* [or *groats*] I will explain below.

Eight marks, then, of new schillings (sixty each) contained one pound of silver. This is sufficiently clear from their composition: they are one-half bronze and one-half silver, and eight marks weigh about two pounds. The old ones weighed the same, but had half the silver content [Latin *valor*]: it took sixteen marks to get a pound of silver, so the ratio of weight to silver content was four to one.

Afterwards, however, when there was a change of government, when the cities were granted the power to mint coinage (and they fully used this privilege) money increased in quantity but not in quality [Latin *bonitas* — *goodness*].[16] A fifth part of silver began to be combined with four parts of bronze in *old schillings*, until it required twenty marks to be changed for a pound of silver.[17] At this stage, since the *new schillings* [i.e., of the reformed value] were now more than twice the worth of the latest schillings, they were made into scots, that were now to be twenty-four [instead of sixty] to the lightweight mark.[18] Thereby a fifth part of the worth [Latin *bonitas*] of the mark was lost.[19] After that, when the new schillings (now made into scots) disappeared since they had been accepted even through the March [of Brandenburg],[20] it was decided to recall them through the [new] valuation of *groats* [Latin *grossi*], that is, to have each groat be the equivalent of three [old, cheaper] schillings.[21] This was a huge mistake and completely beneath the dignity of such a wise gathering of leaders; as if Prussia could not survive without them, although they were not worth more than fifteen pennies each [Latin *denarii*] of the current value of money, when the quantity was overwhelming its valuation [Latin *aestimatio*]. Thus the groats were out of sync with the schillings by being worth a fifth or sixth part less than what they were established to be,[22] and by this fallacious and unfair valuation, they detracted from the dignity of the schilling. Perhaps it was only fitting to take revenge for the injury that schillings had first inflicted on the groats by forcing them to become scots![23]

But woe to you, Prussia! With your collapse, you are paying the price of a badly administered republic! And now, although both the material value and the valuation of your money are vanishing everywhere, still there is no cessation from the coining of money, and even when the expenses [of doing so] are not being met, through which the later coinages would seem to be equivalent of the earlier, and a later coin was always introduced that ruined the quality of the earlier coin, until the valuation of schillings became proportionate to the material worth of the groats, and twenty-four light marks went for one pound of silver. At long last, even such a diminished value of the money should have remained: indeed, there was no thought of formally establishing it. But what had over so long a period of time become the inveterate habit (or license) of adulterating, pilfering, and cheapening the money,[24] has not ceased in our day. For what it later became and what it is today I am ashamed to say. The value has collapsed so much that now *thirty* marks scarcely contain a pound of silver! What will come next, unless we do something? Prussia will be totally empty of gold and silver and will have only copper money. Imports of foreign goods will cease and soon all business dealings as well. What foreign merchant will want to exchange his goods for copper? And finally, what one of our merchants will be able to acquire foreign goods with that same money? But those who are in charge think little of this huge disaster of the Prussian republic, and their most sweet fatherland (to which they owe — in second place, of course, to their piety toward God — not only their occupations but their very lives) allow it to languish and go to ruin, more and more as the days go by, through their spineless negligence.

So then, while Prussian currency, and thus the entire country, suffers from such great problems, only the goldsmiths and people who are expert in judging the quality of metals profit from these miseries. This is because they are good at collecting the old money out of the mix, can melt it down and sell the silver, always getting more silver out of the inexperienced populace. Once those early shillings have completely disappeared, they start to collect the second best, leaving a pile of inferior money left over. This is what leads to that constant complaint people make that the price of gold, silver, the family grocery bill, the cost of services, and anything that anybody needs is going up; but we are blind to the fact that the expensiveness of everything proceeds from the debasement of the money. Everything goes up or down according to the condition of money, and especially gold and silver, whose value we do not determine by bronze or copper but by gold and silver: the point is, gold and silver are a kind of basis upon which the appreciation of money's value [*aestimatio*] depends.

But perhaps someone will object, "A leaner money is more advantageous to human uses: it really helps the poor, by bringing a lower price of groceries and by supplying the other necessities of life more easily, whereas when the money is of higher value, everything becomes more expensive, and tenant farmers and people who have to pay annual rents are burdened more than usual." The people who will applaud this point of view are the ones who have been deprived of their hope of the profits they were planning to make, before their ability to mint money was prohibited, and probably certain merchants and craftsmen might agree: people who won't otherwise lose anything, when they sell their services and goods at the value of gold, and can exchange that for a greater sum of money, the cheaper the money's worth.

But if such persons will only consider the common good [*communis utilitas*], they certainly will not deny that an excellent currency is good not only for the state but for themselves and all classes of people, and that cheap money is harmful. The truth of this is clear, not only for many other reasons but especially thanks to that wise teacher, experience: we see countries that have good money flourishing most of all, and those with poor money declining and perishing. It is no wonder that Prussia was flourishing when one Prussian mark was changed for two Hungarian florins, and when, as I said in the beginning, two Prussian marks and eight scots were exchanged for a half-pound, that is, a (weighted) mark of pure silver. But since then, the money has been cheapening more and more every day, and our country through this pestilence and other catastrophes has been nearly brought to ruin. It is also well known that wherever cheap money is in use, the practice of the better arts and human talents is neglected through laziness, lack of interest and a kind of cowardly idleness, and there is no abundance of anything: nobody has forgotten how inexpensively grain and food could be purchased in Prussia when we still had good money. Now that the currency is debased, we are experiencing a rise in the price of everything useful for human life. And therefore it is clear that cheap money encourages laziness rather than helps anyone's poverty. Nor will an improvement of money burden those who pay a yearly rent, for although they may seem to be paying more than usual for their property, they will also be selling the fruits of their land, their livestock, and that kind of thing for a larger price themselves. The reciprocal give-and-take of buying and selling will be balanced out through the proportionate measurement of the money.

A Plan for Reform

IF IT HAS FINALLY BEEN DETERMINED, then, to rescue, some day, the present disastrous condition of Prussia through a restoration of the currency, we must first of all take care to avoid the confusion that comes from having a variety of mints producing the money. The multiplicity prevents uniformity, and it will be more work to keep a number of mints on the right path than one.... *It would be advantageous therefore for there to be only one common mint for all Prussia,*[25] *in which every type of money would be stamped on one side with the insignia of the lands of Prussia: they should have a crown at the top, so that the superiority of the kingdom would be recognized. On the obverse, the insignia of the duke of Prussia could be seen under the crown above it.*

But if the duke of Prussia refuses this arrangement, and wants to have his own mint ... let two places (at most) be designated, one in the lands of the royal majesty and the other in the territory of the duke.[26] In the former, let money be minted with royal insignia on one side but with [the insignia of] the lands of Prussia on the other, but in the latter mint, let one side have royal insignia and the other the duke's insignia. Let both coinages be subject to the royal authority and be used and accepted throughout the entire land by the order of His Royal Majesty. This measure will have no small impetus toward reconciling those who disagree and toward encouraging the successful pursuit of business operations.

It would be worth the trouble to have both these coinages of the same grain [*granum*], metallic value [*valor*], and monetary value [*aestimatio*], and that they stay that way permanently, through the vigilant supervision of the political authorities, according to the arrangement now to be established.[27] And it would also be important that the authorities in both operations obtain no profit from coining money: let only so much bronze be added that the monetary value exceeds the metallic value just enough to reimburse the cost of making the money, and to remove the temptation to melt it down again.[28]

In order, then, to avoid falling once again into the confusion of our times caused by the mixture of the new money with the old money, it seems imperative to get rid of the old money completely, and let it perish, once the new money has been made; and that this old money then be exchanged for new, according to the proportion of its metallic value. Otherwise, the work of renewing the coinage will be a waste of time, and the resulting confusion perhaps worse than before. Once again, the old money will adulterate the worth of the new money: the mixed money will make the total weigh less than what is proper, and once it has been excessively increased [in quantity], will lead to the problem described above.[29] Now, before this time people have sought to solve this problem by keeping the old money in circulation and simply allowing it a smaller comparative worth in proportion as its metallic value is less or cheaper than that of the new money. But this cannot be done without huge confusion: there is already such a complicated diversity of groats [*grossi*] and schillings [*solidi*] and even pennies [*denarii*] that any given coin can hardly be judged for its value, or be distinguished from other coins. This is how an artificially induced variety of money generates inextricable confusion and increases trouble for merchants and labor contractors, not to mention other problems. Therefore, it will always be preferable to completely abolish the old money when restoring new money. Such a relatively minor loss should always be endured with patience — if we should even consider a "loss" what actually increases profits and brings continual improvement and growth to the republic.

But it is extremely difficult — and, after the catastrophe we have suffered, almost impossible — to restore Prussian money to its original quality. But, although any restoration will take a lot of trouble, nevertheless in the conditions of our time it does seem possible and convenient to effect a renovation, so that at least one pound of silver would go into twenty marks, in the following way: let three pounds of bronze be used for the schillings, along with one pound of silver minus one half-ounce or however much must be allowed for the expenses of minting. Let that molten mass be made into twenty marks, which will be able to pay for one pound (or two-weight marks) of silver. Scots, groats, and obols [i.e., pennies] could then be produced as desired, according to the same formula.

A Comparison of Silver and Gold

IT WAS STATED IN THE BEGINNING that gold and silver are the basis on which the goodness [*bonitas*] of money depends. And what has been said about silver money can also be said, for the most part, about gold. All that remains is to explain, in a brief digression, the rationale involved in exchanging gold and silver. First, we must investigate the method of determining the relative prices of pure gold and pure silver, moving in this way from general to specific and from the simple to the more complex. In fact, the relationship between gold and silver (of the same grade) in the mass[30] is the same as between gold and silver of the same grade when already coined, and again, the relationship of coined gold to mass gold is the same as the relationship of coined silver to mass silver, as long as the proportion of alloy and the weight are the same. Now the purest gold to be found in the coinage we use is in Hungarian florins, which have a minimum admixture of alloy: only just enough, perhaps, as needed to fund the expense of coining the money, and therefore florins are normally exchanged for the equivalent of their weight in pure gold, the dignity [*dignitas*] of the stamped coin making up for the subtraction of gold. It follows, therefore, that the same relationship exists between pure unformed silver and pure unformed gold as between this same kind of silver and Hungarian florins, as long as the weights are kept the same. But 110 Hungarian florins — each of the same and proper weight, that is, of 72 grains — make up 1 pound (I am thinking still of a pound as containing 2 marks of weight). By this criterion we find universally, and in all nations, that one pound of pure gold has as much value as twelve pounds of pure silver. However, we have discovered that once it was *eleven* pounds [of silver] for one [of gold], and thus it appears to have been determined long ago that *ten* Hungarian gold pieces weighed an eleventh part of a pound.[31] But if that same price for the same weight was still in force today, we could have (according to the reasoning here presented) a convenient conformity of Polish and Prussian money: for if 20 marks or thereabouts were to be made from 1 pound of silver, then precisely 2 marks would equal 1 gold piece,[32] the equivalent of 40 Polish groats. But now that it has become an accepted custom in practice that 12 parts of silver are the equal of 1 part of gold, the weight does not match up with the price, so that 10 Hungarian gold pieces can buy a 1 1/11 part of a pound of silver. If, therefore, 20 marks can be made from 1 1/11 pounds of silver, then Polish and Prussian money will be coordinated in value, groat for groat, and 2 Prussian marks will be equivalent to 1 Hungarian gold piece. But the price of silver will be 9 marks[33] and 10 solidi for each ½-pound, or thereabouts.

However, if what people desire is cheapness of money and the destruction of the country, and if this modest restitution and value coordination will seem too difficult to undertake,[34] so that it is decided that 15 Polish groats should remain the worth of 1 mark, and 2 marks 16 scots (i.e., 2 2/3 marks) should remain at the worth of 1 Hungarian gold piece, by the same reckoning it will not be a huge problem for 24 marks to be made from 1 pound of silver.[35] This is what happened not long ago, when 12 marks was still the price of a ½-pound of silver, and 1 Hungarian florin was exchanged for that much money. This is mentioned for the sake of an example, and to suggest a way to proceed. There are countless methods for configuring a monetary system, and it is not possible to explain them all. Common consensus, arrived at after careful deliberation, will be able to determine whatever seems most suitable for the republic. But if our money is properly related to the Hungarian florin and has been correctly made, other [kinds of] florins will also be set in correlation with them, according to their gold and silver contents.

This seems to be enough on the subject of restoring currency; I hope that with the foregoing I have clearly explained in what ways its worth [*dignitas*] has fallen, and how it can be restored.

Epilogue on the Restoration of Money

THE FOLLOWING POINTS need to be taken into account in understanding the repair and preservation of money.

First: let there be no renewal without the slow deliberation and unanimous decree of the rulers.

Second: let there be only one place set aside, if possible, for an official mint, and let such a mint produce money with a stamp on it, not in the name of one city alone, but for the whole country, together with its symbols. The Polish money demonstrates the significance of this recommendation, for it is only because of this that it keeps its value over so much territory.

Third: when new money is being minted and distributed, let the old money be taken out of circulation and abolished.

Fourth: let it be invariably, and without any compromise perpetually, observed that twenty marks and no more be made from one pound of pure silver, with only so much being subtracted as can cover the expenses of the minting. In this way, Prussian money will be proportionate to Polish money, and twenty Prussian groats as well as twenty Polish groats will be the equivalent of one Prussian mark.

Fifth: that the excess production of money be avoided.

Sixth: that the money be simultaneously produced in all its denominations. Scots or groats, solids [schillings], and obols [pennies] should all be minted.

With respect to the amount of alloy: whether groats or solids are produced, or even silver *denarii* which can add up to a *ferto* [one fourth of a mark — German *Viertel*] or half-mark, or even a whole mark, let it be decided according to the wishes of those who are concerned, provided only that moderation be exercised and that a decision is made that can have lasting effectiveness.

Let there be provision for *obols* as well, since they have simply too little value now, with an entire mark's worth of them containing barely more silver than in one groat.

A final difficulty arises from the existence of contracts and obligations made before and after the renewal of the money. A way should be found for solving these issues that does not overly burden the contracting parties. An example of how this was done in earlier times is presented on the following page.[36]

Appendices

Appendix I

Nicolaus Copernicus Was Far More Than A Scientific Icon

by Jonathan Decker

NICOLAUS COPERNICUS is a scientific icon. He, of course, discovered that the Earth revolves around the Sun. Copernicus also wrote a little known essay entitled *On the Minting of Money*. Last month, Laissez Faire Books issued a lucid, meticulously retranslated, new edition of this formerly obscure work.

On the Minting of Money presents the case for the classical gold standard. It is beautifully written and as relevant to 2014 as it was to 1526. Let's hope the monetary authorities listen this time.

Copernicus's insights on monetary policy are as profound as were his astronomical insights, although not yet assimilated by the culture. Two well recognized modern proponents of restoring a 21st century gold standard, Ralph Benko and Charles Kadlec, contributors to Forbes.com Opinions and advisors to the Lehrman Institute's highly regarded web-based compendium on all things gold standard, served as editors.

An erudite classicist, Professor Gerald Malsbary, provided the translation. Reagan Gold Commissioner (and founder/chairman of the Lehrman Institute) Lewis E. Lehrman also contributes to the foreword.

Lehrman: "the mathematical proofs that Ptolemy used to show the Earth as the center of the solar system were superseded by the verifiable calculations of Copernicus. The Earth did revolve regularly around the sun, not the other way around as Ptolemy's detailed calculations suggested. Thus, we live in a Copernican world, preceded by the Copernican revolution. What Copernicus established as the scientific rules governing money are as true today as are the path breaking rules of Copernicus governing the solar system."

Benko, in an introduction, observes that "the gold standard has unrivaled intellectual pedigree" and, with Copernicus's contribution to monetary policy now translated and readily available, "the elegance of the provenance of the gold standard hereby is restored to its deserved level."

Copernicus explains how the steady debasement of the Prussian currency eroded the value of individual earnings and harmed the economy. He writes,

"We see countries that have good money flourishing most of all, and those with poor money declining and perishing. ... [S]ince then our money has been cheapening more and more every day, and our country through this pestilence has been nearly brought to ruin."

Copernicus adds, "now that the currency is debased, we are experiencing a rise in the price of everything useful for human life. And therefore it is clear that cheap money encourages laziness rather than helps anyone's poverty."

Copernicus' warning against the debasement of a currency anticipates what has occurred in American monetary policy. A dollar today is worth a mere 5 cents of what a dollar the gold-defined dollar was worth in 1913. When the dollar has sagged — especially in the last 12 years — the American and world economy have stagnated. Just as Copernicus observed in his day and his nation.

This thin but elegant volume's co-editor Charles Kadlec previously noted, in one of his Forbes.com columns, at the Federal Reserve's 2% target inflation rate individuals who cannot keep up with inflation will lose one third of the value of their savings within twenty years. Copernicus observed that "countries that have good money flourish." As did the United States did under the classical gold standard.

According to Forbes.com columnist Nathan Lewis, in a column entitled 'The Correlation Between the Gold Standard and Stupendous Growth Is Clear', the best period of economic growth in the history of the United States (and, perhaps the world) occurred when the classical gold standard was in effect.

Economic growth in the U.S. has turned stagnant during the very period in which our Federal Reserve Notes have been steadily debased. Analysts at the Bank of England described this trend in Financial Stability Report No. 13. As summarized in another Forbes.com article by Kadlec, stronger economic growth was common under both the classical gold and gold-exchange standards.

As composer Herman Hupfeld unforgettably wrote: "The fundamental things don't change as time goes by." Copernicus' Essay on Money is an insightful read, and a perfect virtual stocking stuffer. Let us hope that this excellent edition will lead to a monetary "Copernican Revolution" via a closer look at how the gold standard could be an important factor in creating a climate of equitable prosperity for the world.

Originally featured in the Forbes online Capital Flows section.

December 12, 2013.

Appendix II

A Brief History of Money

by Ralph Benko

"[T]he study of monetary questions is one of the great causes of insanity."

– U.S. Senator and National Monetary Commission Chairman Nelson Aldrich.

Introduction

Money

MONEY IS A TECHNOLOGY designed to facilitate commerce and investment. Money was primarily developed by scientists, not economists, although first definitively defined by that great economist William Stanley Jevons.

Economists study money. Scientists defined and engineered it.

When the notorious Scottish economist John Law meddled in French monetary policy, he infamously muddled it, destroying France financially.

What is Money?

Wikipedia summarizes the consensus well:

"In Money and the Mechanism of Exchange (1875), William Stanley Jevons famously analyzed money in terms of four functions: a medium of exchange, a common measure of value (or unit of account), a standard of value (or

standard of deferred payment), and a store of value. By 1919, Jevons's four functions of money were summarized in the couplet:

Money's a matter of functions four,
A Medium, a Measure, a Standard, a Store.

"This couplet would later become widely popular in macroeconomics textbooks. Most modern textbooks now list only three functions, that of the medium of exchange, unit of account, and store of value."

Not for nothing did U.S. Senator Nelson Aldrich — while reporting, in 1909, on the observations of his National Monetary Commission, in a speech before the Economic Club of New York — archly quote McLeod to the effect that:

"the study of monetary questions is one of the great causes of insanity."

This was almost certainly a swipe at free silver demagogue and presidential candidate William Jennings "You shall not crucify mankind upon a cross of gold" Bryan.

Not so incidentally, let us recall quantum physicist Niels Bohr's comment to Wolfgang Pauli:

"We are all agreed that your theory is crazy. The question that divides us is whether it is crazy enough to have a chance of being correct."

As it happens, money has a sterling scientific provenance.

Money's Provenance

Copernicus

Money's modern scientific provenance goes back at least to Nicholas Copernicus, the very same savant who persuaded the Earth to orbit the Sun instead of the Sun orbiting the Earth as previously believed.

In 1526, yes, nearly 500 years ago, Copernicus wrote a brilliant treatise *On the Minting of Money*. It was my arcane privilege to serve as the lead co-editor of what may be its most esteemed modern translation.

Copernicus warned:

> *"Although there are countless maladies that are forever causing the decline of kingdoms, princedoms, and republics, the following four (in my judgment) are the most serious: civil discord, a high death rate, sterility of the soil, and the debasement of the coinage. The first three are so obvious that everybody recognizes the damage they cause; but the fourth one, which has to do with money, is noticed by only a few very thoughtful people, since it does not operate all at once and at a single blow, but gradually overthrows governments and in a hidden, insidious way."*

He went on to observe:

> *"Money, or 'coinage', is gold or silver that has been specially marked — in accordance with policy established by any government or head of government — for the purpose of reckoning the prices of things that are bought and sold.*
>
> *"Money is therefore a kind of common 'measuring stick' for the valuation of things. Now, whatever is taken as a measure has to be stable — must keep to a fixed limit.*

Otherwise, public order will necessarily be disturbed, and the buyers and sellers of things will be cheated many times over, just as if basic measures of length [Latin ulna, or ell], bulk measure [Latin modius, or peck], or weight did not have a fixed quantity.

"Now, I think that the relevant measure here is the valuation [Latin aestimatio] of the money as such, and, although this is founded in the quality of the metal it is made of, nevertheless, money's material or metallic value [Latin valor] must be distinguished from its valuation as money [aestimatio]; for money can be valued more in itself than the material it is composed of and vice versa [i.e., its material value may be more than its actual valuation].

"It is necessary for money to be established: even though exchange could also take place simply by weights of gold or silver alone (since, by universal human consent, gold and silver are everywhere highly valued).

"Nevertheless, money is needed for two reasons: first, because of the inconvenience of always having to carry around heavy weights of metal, and second, because the real value of the metals is not easily grasped by everyone at a glance. Thus it has become customary to mark money with a public seal, by means of which the proper amount of gold or silver is indicated as present in each coin, and that the public authority is to be trusted in this.

...

"The [material] value of money is lessened in many ways: either through defect of material alone, namely, when more bronze is mixed with silver than is right for that particular weight of coin; or through the loss of [total] weight of the coin, even though the proportion of bronze to silver is correct; or (and this is the worst case) through both of these defects

occurring at the same time; finally, the value can just diminish on its own through usage, over a long passage of time, and this is the only reason for making new money.

"The evidence of this happening is, if the silver in the money is found to be significantly less than what can be bought with it — and this is rightly considered debasement [or poverty: Latin penuria] of the currency."

The Prussian nobles who Copernicus was addressing did not heed his wise advice. They eventually suffered the fate he predicted.

Newton

In addition to observing an apple's fall and founding modern physics, Sir Isaac Newton served, professionally, as the Master of the Royal Mint of Great Britain toward the end of the 17th and beginning of the 18th century.

Per the Royal Mint itself:

"When Sir Isaac Newton came to the Royal Mint Britain's finances were approaching crisis, with up to one in ten circulating coins believed to be forged. His vision of matchless quality led him to root out and prosecute notorious counterfeiters, improve assaying techniques (the way coin quality is checked), and refine weights and measures to standards never seen before.

"In 1699 Newton became Master of the Mint. After overseeing the new coinage for the accession of Queen Anne in 1702 he also supervised the huge task of bringing Scottish coinage into line with English coinage, following the Union of England and Scotland in 1707. Thanks to

Newton's vision, Royal Mint coins remain unrivaled in their accuracy and purity to this day."

How great a figure was Newton?

Just for a moment, consider the last words of the first celebrity economist, John Maynard Keynes, delivered posthumously by his brother, Geoffrey, singing the praises of Newton in the 1940's.

"Newton was not the first of the age of reason. He was the last of the magicians, the last of the Babylonians and Sumerians, the last great mind which looked out on the visible and intellectual world with the same eyes as those who began to build our intellectual inheritance rather less than 10,000 years ago. Isaac Newton, a posthumous child born with no father on Christmas Day, 1642, was the last wonderchild to whom the Magi could do sincere and appropriate homage."

And per Christianity Today:

"Even in Newton's lifetime, his contemporaries' adulation verged on worship. Following his death in April 1727, Newton lay in state in Westminster Abbey for a week. At the funeral, his pall was borne by three earls, two dukes, and the Lord Chancellor. Voltaire observed, 'He was buried like a king who had done well by his subjects.'

"No scientist before or since has been so revered and interred with such high honor.

"Who was this man whose stature has dominated the scientific landscape for three centuries? Why did his achievements have such an impact on society? What role did Newton's faith play in his life and work?"

…

"For Newton the world of science was by no means the whole of life. He spent more time on theology than on science; indeed, he wrote about 1.3 million words on biblical subjects. Yet this vast legacy lay hidden from public view for two centuries until the auction of his nonscientific writings in 1936.

"Newton's understanding of God came primarily from the Bible, which he studied for days and weeks at a time. He took a special interest in miracles and prophecy, calculating dates of Old Testament books and analyzing their texts to discover their authorship. In a manuscript on rules for interpreting prophecy, Newton noted the similar goals of the scientist and the prophecy expositor: simplicity and unity."

Although the Sermon on the Mountain contains an aphorism holding that you cannot serve both God and money, Newton proves a clear exception to that rule.

What was Newton's Monetary Legacy?

A happy accident by Newton led to the gold standard, a monetary system which helped Great Britain prosper, proving instrumental in Britain's becoming a dominant world power. Wikipedia:

"Great Britain accidentally adopted a de facto gold standard in 1717 when Sir Isaac Newton, then-master of the Royal Mint, set the exchange rate of silver to gold too low, thus causing silver coins to go out of circulation.

"A formal gold specie standard was first established in 1821, when Britain adopted it following the introduction of the gold sovereign by the new Royal Mint at Tower Hill in 1816.

"As Great Britain became the world's leading financial and commercial power in the 19th century, other states increasingly adopted Britain's monetary system.

...

"The gold specie standard came to an end in the United Kingdom and the rest of the British Empire with the outbreak of World War I."

Contemporaneously with Newton, John Law, a Scottish economist, introduced a paper money standard (what some today call "fiat") in France. This led to a speculative bubble, horrendous inflation, and both France's and Law's financial ruin.

Per Wikipedia:

"[Law] served as Controller General of Finances under the Duke of Orleans, who was regent for the juvenile Louis XV of France. In 1716, Law set up a private Banque Générale in France. A year later it was nationalized at his request and renamed as Banque Royale. ...

"Law also set up and directed the Mississippi Company, funded by the Banque Royale. Its chaotic collapse has been compared to the 17th-century tulip mania in Holland. The Mississippi bubble coincided with the South Sea bubble in England, which allegedly took ideas from it. Law as a gambler would win card games by mentally calculating odds.... The term 'millionaire' was coined for beneficiaries of Law's scheme.

...

"Speculation gave way to panic as people flooded the market with future shares trading as high as 15,000 livres per

share, while the shares themselves remained at 10,000 livres each.

"By May 1720, prices fell to 4,000 livres per share, a 73 per cent decrease within a year. The rush to convert paper money to coins led to sporadic bank hours and riots..."

The descent of a relatively unknown man came as fast as his rise, leaving an economic power vacuum. Law's theories live on 300 years later and 'captured many key conceptual points which are very much a part of modern monetary theorizing.'

Priestley

Fast forward again, now toward the mid-to-late 1700s. One of the first great chemists, Joseph Priestley, the discoverer of oxygen and the inventor of carbonation (an invention upon which our soft-drink industry is based) wrote extensively and eruditely on the gold standard, providing an extensive lecture on the mechanics of money later published in his Lectures on History and General Philosophy (1793).

Per Wikipedia:

"Lectures on History and General Policy (1788) is the published version of a set of lectures on history and government given by the 18th-century British polymath Joseph Priestley to the students of Warrington Academy.

"The Lectures cover an array of topics — 'forms of government, the feudal system, the rise of corporations, law, agriculture, commerce, the arts, finance and taxation, colonies, manners, population, war and peace' — demonstrating how all-encompassing Priestley believed the study of history to be.

"Priestley offers a version of history in which all events are 'an exhibition of the ways of God.' Studying history and nature, according to Priestley, 'leads us to the knowledge of his perfections and of his will.' Understanding history thus allows one to comprehend the natural laws God established and the perfection towards which they allow the world to tend. This millennial outlook is tied together with Priestley's belief in scientific progress and the improvement of the human race."

Conclusion

And there you have a potted history of the scientists who invented money as we knew it and know it today: Copernicus, Newton, Priestley.

I have treated you to the scientific provenance of the key makers of money, with brief detours to the distinguished monetary economist Jevons, a passing reference to the first celebrity economist, John Maynard Keynes, and a revelation of the notorious economist John Law, proponent of promiscuously issued paper money with its attendant catastrophic debasement.

Contemplating the contributions of distinguished scientists, coupled with brief forays to three influential economists, gives us insight into the potential future of money, governance and the law.

Let us reprise the view of the great discoverer of oxygen who offers: "A version of history in which all events are 'an exhibition of the ways of God;'" studying history and nature, according to Priestley, to lead "us to the knowledge of [God's] perfections and of [God's] will".

Let us reprise the quest of the great Newton, who sought, both as to prophecy and science, simplicity and unity.

Adapted from remarks presented at the Government Blockchain Association's The Future of Money, Governance and the Law, event at the National Press Club.

January 27, 2022. Revised July 2, 2025.

Appendix III

LATIN ORIGINAL[37]

Monetae Cudendae Ratio

QUANQUAM INNUMERE PESTES sunt quibus regna, principatus, et respublice decrescere solent, hæc tamen quatuor (meo judicio) potissime sunt: discordia, mortalitas, terre sterilitas et monete vilitas. Tria prima adeo evidentia sunt, ut nemo ita esse nesciat, sed quartum quod ad monetam attinet a paucis et nonnisi cordatissimis consideratur, quia non uno impetu simul, sed paulatim, occulta quadam ratione respublicas evertit.

Est autem moneta aurum vel argentum signatum, qua pretia emptibiliurn vendibiliumque rerum numerantur secundum cujusvis reipublice vel gubernantis ipsum institutum. Est ergo moneta tanquam mensura quædam communis æstimationum. Oportet autem id quod mensura esse debet firmum semper ac statum servare modum. Alioquin necesse est confundi ordinationem reipublice, ementes quoque et vendentes multipliciter defraudari, quemadmodum si ulna, modius, pondusve certam quantitatem non servet. Hanc igitur mensuram æstimationem puto ipsius monete, que etsi in bonitate materie fundetur, oportet tamen valorem ab estitnatione discerni; potest enim pluris estimari moneta quam ejus qua constat materia et e converso.

Causa vero constitutionis monete necessaria est; quamvis enim solo pondere auri et argenti rerum commutatio fieri potuisset, ex quo communi hominum consensu aurum et argentum ubique in pretio habeatur, sed tamen propter multam incommoditatem afferendorum semper ponderum, quodque non statim auri et argenti sinceritas deprehendatur ab omnibus, institutum est publico sigillo monetam signari, quo significetur justam auri vel argenti quantitatem inesse, et fides adhibeatur auctoritati.

Solet etiam monete et maxime argente es commisceri propter duas (ut existimo) causas, videlicet quo minus exposita sit insidiis expilantium et conflantium ipsum quod futurum esset si ex sincero argento constaret. Secunda, quod massa argenti in minutas partes et scrupulos nummorum fracta retineat, cum ere admixto, convenientem magnitudinem: potest superaddi et tertia, ne scilicet continuo usu detrita citius pereat, sed fulcitamento eris diuturnior perseveret.

Justa autem et equa monete estimatio est, quando paulo minus auri vel argenti continet quam pro ipsa ematur: utpote quantum pro expensis dumtaxat monetariorum oportuerit deduci. Debet enim signum ipsi materie aliquam addere dignitatem.

Vilescit hec ut plurimum propter nimiam multitudinem, utpote si tanta argenti copia in monetam transierit quoadusque argenti massa ab hominibus magis quam moneta desideretur: perit nempe hoc modo dignitas monete, quando per ipsam tantum argenti non licet emere quantum ipsa pecunia continet, sentiaturque major profectus eliquando argentum in monete destructionem, cujus remedium est non amplius monetam cudere donec se ipsam coequaverit, reddaturque carior argento.

Valor quoque multis modis depravatur, vel propter defectum materie solum, quando scilicet sub eodem pondere monete plus quam oportet eris commiscetur argento, vel propter defectum ponderis, quamvis justam habeat eris cum argento admixtionem: vel, quod pessimum est, propter utramque simul; deficit etiam ultro valor ac longo usu deteritur, propter quod solum instaurari ac innovari debet. Cujus signum est, si argentum in moneta in notabili quantitate minus reperitur quam pro ipsa emptum, in quo merito penuria monete intelligitur.

Premissis generaliter de moneta expositis, speciatim ad Prussianam descendamus, ostendentes primum quomodo in tantam levitatern pervenerit.

Transit autem sub nominibus marcharum, scotorum, etc., et sunt sub eisdem nominibus etiam pondura. Nam marcha ponderis est libra media. At marcha numeri constat solidis LX: quæ omnia vulgo nota sunt.

Verum ne equivocatio numeri et ponderis obscuritatem pariat, ubicumque deinceps marcha nominabitur, de numero intelligatur; nomine vero libre, pondus duarum marcharum, pro selibra vero marcham ponderis accipe.

Invenimus igitur in antiquis recessibus ac litterarum monumentis quod sub magistratu Conradi de Jungingen, hoc est proxime ante bellum Tanebergense, emebatur selibra, id est marcha argenti puri, marchis pruthenicalibus duabus et scotis VIII, quando videlicet tribus partibus argenti puri quarta pars eris admiscebatur, et ex libra dimidia ejus masse solidos CXII faciebant. Quibus tertia pars adjecta, et sunt solidi XXXVII et tertia pars unius solidi, facit totam summam solidorum CXLVIII et duorum d. pendentem libre unius bessem duas tertias hoc est scotos scilicet argenti XXXII que procul dubio tres partes (et sunt libra media argenti puri) continebit. Sed jam dictum est pretium ejus fuisse solidos CXL in selibras. Reliquum vero quod in IX solidos et tertia deerat estimatio monete supplevit. Erat itaque ejus estimatio cum valore convenienter continuata.

Hujus generis nummisimata sunt Henrici, Ulrici, et Conradi, que interdum reperiuntur adhuc in thesauris. Deinde post cladem Prussie et bellum supradictum reipublice in dies magis ac magis in moneta apparere. Nam Henrici solidi, aspectu quidem similes supradictis, non amplius reperiuntur habere quam tres quintas argenti. Crescebatque error hic donec inverso ordine ceptum est tribus partibus eris quartam argenti misceri, ut jam non argenti moneta, sed cuprea rectius diceretur, pondus tamen retinebat solidorum CXII in selibra. Cum autem minime conveniat novam ac bonam monetam introducere antiqua viliore remanente, quanto hic magis erratum est vetere meliore remanente viliorem novam introducendoque non solum infecit antiquam, sed, ut ita dicam, expugnavit. Cui errori dum sub magistratu Michaelis Rusdorff obviare vellent ac monetam in pristinum meliorem statum reducere, cudebant novos solidos quos nunc grossos vocamus; sed cum antiqui viliores non viderentur sine jactura aboleri posse una cum novis insigni errore permanserunt.

Transibantque duo solidi antiqui pro uno novo, factumque tunc est, quod duplex marcha plebi ingereretur novorum videlicet solidorum et antiquorum. Illorum marcha nova sive bona, horum vero antiqua sive levis, solidorum utrobique sexaginta. Oboli vero in suo usu manebant. Ita ut pro solido antiquo sex duntaxat commutarentur, pro novo vero XII. Nam ab initio duodecim obolorum fuisse solidum facile conjici potest. Sicut enim quindenum numerum vulgo mandel vocamus, ita in plerisque Germanie terris vox illa schilling pro duodenario numero durat. Perseveravit autem novorum solidorum appellatio usque ad memoriam nostram: quomodo demum grossi facti sunt inferius dicam.

Novorum igitur solidorum marche VIII per sexaginta libram unam puri argenti continebant: quod ex eorum compositione satis apparet. Constant enim ex dimidio eris et altera medietate argenti et eorum marche VIII per LX pendent prope libras duas. Antiqui vero pondere, ut dictum est, pares illis, valore ex dimidio; cum enim quartam solummodo partem argenti haberent, marche XVI e libra argenti puri veniebant, pendentes quadruplum. Postea vero mutato statu patrie, cum civitatibus esset cudendi monetam concessa potestas, ipseque novum exequerentur privilegium, crevit pecunia multitudine, non autem bonitate. Cepitque quatuor partibus eris quinta argenti in solidis antiquis misceri donec marche XX argenti libra commutarentur. Sicque novi illi solidi cum jam meliores essent plus quam duplo, solidis recentibus facti sunt scoti ut jam XXIIII pro marcha levi computarentur: periit ergo quinta pars bonitatis monete in marcha. Postea vero quam evanescerent novi solidi jam scoti facti eo quod eciam per Marchiam essent accepti, placuit eos grossorum estimatione revocare, hoc est sub solidis tribus, maximo errore et tanto procerum consilio prorsus indigno, perinde ac si Prussia sine illis esse non posset, quamvis non essent meliores denariis quindecim tunc currentis monete, ubi jam multitudo etiam premebat estimatione ipsius. Dissidebant ergo grossi cum solidis in quinta vel sexta parte minus valentes a constituto et fallaci et iniqua estimatione detrahebant dignitati solidorum.

Oportebat fortassis injuria sic vindicari quam solidi grossis prius intulerant coegerantque eos scotos fieri. Sed ve tibi Prussia que tuo proh dolor! interitu male administrate reipublice penas pendis. Igitur estimatione simul et valore pecunie passim evanescentibus, a fabricatione tamen monete plane cessatum non est, et expensis non suppetentibus quibus equivalens priori redderetur posterior, semper priori pejor superinducta est quæ bonitatem precedentis oppressit et extinxit, quoad solidorum estimatio cum valore grossorum proporcionaliter convenerit et marche XXIV leves pro una libra cesserit argenti.

Debuerant autem jam tandem saltem reliquie tantille dignitatis monete permansisse, ex quo de ejus instauratione meditatum non est. Sed que tantisper inolevit consuetudo sive licencia adulterandi, expilandi et inficiendi monetam cessare non potuit nec in hunc diem cessat. Nam qualis postea prodierit et in quo statu nunc sit, pudet ac dolet dicere. In tantam enim vilitatem hodie collapsa est, ut XXX marche unam libram argenti vix contineant. Quid autem restat si non succurratur, nisi ut deinceps Prussia, auro et argento vacua, monetam mere cupream habeat. Unde peregrinarum mercium invectiones, omnesque negociationes brevi sint periture. Quis enim externorum mercatorum merces suas moneta cuprea commutare volet? Quis denique nostratium in peregrinis terris eadem moneta exoticas merces comparare poterit? Hanc tamen ingentem reipublice prussiane cladem hi quorum interest contempti despiciunt et dulcissimam sibi patriam cui post pietatem in Deum nedum officii plurimum, sed eciam ipsam vitam debent, in dies magis ac magis supina negligencia miserabiliter labi ac periri sinunt.

Cum ergo tantis viciis laboret prussiana moneta et per eam tota patria, soli aurifices et hi qui bonitatem metalli callent ejus erumnis fruuntur. Colligunt enim ex mixta pecunia antiquam ex qua eliquatum argentum vendunt, plus semper argenti cum moneta mixta ab imperito vulgo recipientes: at postquam antiqui illi solidi jam penitus evanescant, eliguntur proximo meliores relicto pecuniarum acervo deteriori. Hinc illa vulgaris et perpetua querimonia aurum, argentum annonam, familie mercedem, opificum operam et quidquid in humanis usibus est solitum, transcendere precium; sed oscitantes non expendimus omnium rerum charitatem ex vilitate monete provenire. Crescunt enim ac decrescunt etiam ad monete conditionem: presertim aurum et argentum que non ere vel cupro, sed auro et argento, appreciamus. Nam aurum et argentum dicimus esse tanquam basim monete cui incubat ejus estimatio.

At contendet fortasse aliquis exilem monetam usibus humanis commodiorem esse: nempe subvenientem paupertati hominum, reddentem levi pretio annonam et cetera vite mortalium necessaria facilius suppeditantem; per bonam autem monetam omnia chariora reddi, colonos ac censu annuo oneratos preter solitum gravari. Laudabunt hanc sententiam, spe lucri privati, quibus hactenus permissa est cudendi monetam facultas, non fortassis mercatores et opifices quibus nihil propterea perit, eam improbabunt, quum quidem ad auri valorem merces et res suas vendunt, et, quo moneta est exilior, eo majori pecuniarum numero eas commutant. Verum si communem utilitatem respicient, negare utique non poterunt prestantem monetam non modo reipublice, verum etiam sibi ac omnium hominum ordini salutarem, exiguam vero perniciosam esse. Quod cum multis rationibus satis perspicuum sit, etiam ipsa experiencia rerum magistra verum esse dicimus: videmus quippe eas terras potissimum florere que bonam monetam habent, decrescere autem et perire que deteriore utuntur: floruit nimirum et Prussia tunc quando una marcha pruthenicalis duobus florenis ungaricis emebatur et quando, ut premissum est, due marche pruthenice et VIII scoti selibra, id est marcha argenti puri, commutabantur. Interim vero vilescente in dies magis ac magis moneta decrescit et patria nostra atque hac peste et aliis calamitatibus usque ad ultimum pene funus perducta est.

Constat preterea ipsa loca que bona moneta utuntur, artibus et opificibus egregiis nec non et rerum affluencia pollere; ac contra, ubi vilis moneta in usu est, ignavia, desidia ac resupinato ocio tam bonarum artium quam ingeniorum culturam negligere atque omnium etiam rerum abundantiam interire. Nondum memoriam hominum excessit frumenta et annonam minori pecuniarum numero in Prussia empta fuisse cum adhuc bona moneta uteretur. Nunc autem, ea vilescente, omnium rerum que ad victum et humanum usum pertinent precium ascendere experimur. Ex quo perspicuum esse potest levem monetam desidiam magis alere quam paupertati hominum subvenire; nec magnopere monete exaltatio censuales gravare poterit qui, si plus solito suo dominio pendere videantur, fructus terre pecora et id genus rerum suarum majori eciam pretio sunt vendituri. Reciprocam enim dandi accipiendique vicissitudinem proportionata monete mensura compensabit.

Si igitur calamitosam hactenus Prussiam monete restauratione jam tandem aliquando restituere placet, cavenda imprimis erit confusio ex varietate diversarum officinarum in quibus cudenda est proveniens. Multiplicitas enim uniformatem impedit majorisque negotii est, plures officinas in officio rectitudinis conservari quam unam. Duo igitur ad summum designentur loca: unus in terris regie majestatis; alter in ditione principis. In primo cudatur rnoneta que ex uno latere insignis regalibus, ex altero terrarum Prussie signetur. In secunda autem officina ex uno latere insigniis regiis, ex altero vero nummismate principis signetur, ut utraque moneta imperio regio subsit et sue majestatis mandato in usu totius regni sit et accepta. Que res ad animorum conciliationem et negociationum communionem non parum ponderis est habitura.

Opere precium autem erit quod he due monete unius sint grani, valoris et estimationis et vigili cura prematum reipublice juxta ordinationem nunc instituendain perpetuo perseverent. Et quod principes utrinque nihil lucri ex monete cussione sentiant, sed tantum duntaxat eris addatur ut ipsa estimatio valorem excedat, ut impendiorum jactura sarciri possit et conflandi monetam adimatur occasio.

Ut item in hujus nostri temporis confusionem quam commixtio nove monete cum antiqua peperit, deinceps non incidamus, necessarium videtur ut exorta nova, vetus aboleatur ac prorsus intereat, et juxta proportionem valoris sui in officinis pro nova commutetur. Alioquin inanis erit renovande monete opera, et confusio posterior fortassis pejor priore. Inficiet enim denuo antiqua nove monete dignitatem: mixta equidem reddet summam a justo pondere deficientem et nimium multiplicatam sequetur que dicta est superius incommoditas. Cui si quis adhuc obviandum arbitretur per hoc videlicet ut remanentia vetera nummismata tanti minoris estimentur comparatione nove monete quantum eorum valor deterior est aut exilior; sed hoc sine magno errore fieri non poterit. Tanta enim est nunc, tum grossorum et solidorum, tum etiam denariorum multiplex diversitas, ut singula nummismata juxta conditionem valoris sui estimari et ab invicem discerni vix possent. Quo fit ut inducta monete varietas confusionem generaret inextricabilem, ac negociantibus et contrahentibus labores, molestias atque alia incommoda augeret. Itaque melius semper erit veterem monetam in reparatione recentis penitus abolere. Oportebit enim tantillum damnum semel equanimiter pati, si modo damnum dici possit unde uberior fructus et utilitas magis constans nascitur ac respublica incrementum sumit.

Monetam vero prussianam in primam illam dignitatem erigere difficillimum est et post tantum casum forte impossibile; tum quevis ejus reparatio res sit non parvi negotii, pro horum tamen temporum conditione commode renovari posse videtur, ut saltem ad XX marchas libra argenti redeat, hac ratione: pro solidis sumantur eris libræ tres, argenti vero puri libra una minus uncia media vel quantum pro expensis detrahendum sit. Confletur massa ex qua marchæ XX fiant que in emptione valebunt libram unam, id est duas marchas argenti. Eadem ratione etiam fieri possunt scoti seu grossi et oboli, prout placuerit.

De Argenti Ad Aurum Comparatione

SUPERIUS DICTUM est aurum et argentum esse basim in qua residet bonitas monete. Et que de moneta argenti exposita sunt, possunt etiam pro majori parte ad auream referri. Reliquum est ut ex transverso auri et argenti commutandi rationem exponamus. Primum igitur investigare oportet que sit ratio appreciationis meri auri ad argentum merum sive purum: ut de genere in specie et a simplicibus ad composita descendamus. Porro eadem est ratio auri et argenti informium, que signatorum in eodem gradu, ac rursus eadem ratio auri signati ad informe, que argenti signati ad argentum informe sub eodem gradu mixtionis et pondere. Purissimum autem aurum quod apud nos signatum reperitur, sunt floreni ungarici; hi namque minimum habent admixtionis et tantum forte quantum oportuerat pro expensis deduci in monetariis, unde rite commutantur pro mero auro sub eodem pondere, dignitate sigili supplente defectum florenorum. Sequitur ergo eamdem esse rationem argenti puri informis ad aurum purum informe et ejusdem argenti ad florenos ungaricos, ponderibus non mutatis. At floreni ungarici CX justi et æqualis ponderis per grana videlicet LXXII, implent libram unam (libram semper intelligo que continet marchas duas ponderis). Hoc argumento invenimus communiter apud omnes gentes libram unam auri puri tantum valere, quantum argenti puri libre XII. Invenimus tamen et XI libras olim pro una auri, quam ob causam ab antiquo constitutum esse videtur ut aurei ungarici X appendant libre partem undecimam: quod si sub eo pondere idem pretium hodie duraret, expeditam haberemus conformitatem monete polonice et pruthenice secundum expositam rationem: factis enim XX marcis circiter ex libra una argenti, provenirent ad amussim pro aureo marche due, loco XL grossorum polonicalium. Sed postea quam usu receptum sit, ut XII partes argenti sint pro una auri, dissidet pondus cum pretio ut X aurei ungaricales redimant libram unam argenti et undecimam partem libre. Si igitur ex libra argenti et ejus undecima parte fiant marche viginti, erunt polona et prussiana monete recta ratione coequate, grossus ad grossum, et marche due pruthenice pro aureo ungaricali. Sed pretium argenti erit in selibras singulas marche VIII et solidi X, aut circiter.

Verum si utique vilitas nionete et patrie interitus placeat ac ardua nimis videbitur tantilla restitutio et adequatio, visumque fuerit ut XV grossi polonici maneant pro marcha, et pro aureo ungaricali marche due scoti XVI; id quoque jam dictis modis non magno negotio fiet, si marche XXIV ex argenti libra fiant. Ita sane contigit nuper quando adhuc marche XII pretium essent in singulas selibras argenti et pro tanta pecunia florenis ungaricis commutabantur. Hic gratia exempli et pro manuductione dicta sunt. Nam infiniti sunt modi constitutionis monete, nec est possibile explicare omnes, sed communis consensus matura deliberatione poterit hoc vel illud definire, prout accommodatissimum videbitur reipublice. Quod si moneta ad florenum ungaricum recte se habuerit et erratum non fuerit, facile etiam alii floreni juxta continentiam auri et argenti ad illorum comparationem taxabuntur.

Hec de monete reparatione dixisse sufficiat, ut dumtaxat intelligatur quibus modis ceciderit dignitas ejus et quomodo reduci possit, quod ex supradictis perspicuum esse spero.

Epilogus Reductionis Monete

CIRCA REPARATIONEM et conservacionem monete hec consideranda videntur:

Primum, ne absque maturo procerum consilio et unanimi decreto moneta novetur.

Secundum, ut unus dumtaxat locus officine monetarie, si fieri potest, deputetur, ubi non unius civitatis nomine, sed tocius terre cum ipsius insigniis fieret, hujus sentencie efficaciam moneta polonica demonstrat que propter hoc solum retinet estimationem suam in tanta terrarum amplitudine.

Tertium, ut in publicacione nove monete interdicatur et aboleatur antiqua.

Quartum, ut inviolabiliter et immutabiliter perpetuo observetur quod XX marche dumtaxat et non amplius fiant ex libra una puri argenti, dempto eo quod pro expensis opificii deduci oportet. Ita nempe prussiana moneta proporcionabitur polonice, ut viginti grossi prussiani simul ac polonici marcham pruthenicam constituant.

Quintum, ut caveatur a nimia monete multitudine.

Sextum, ut in omni specie sua simul prodeat moneta: hoc est ut scoti sive grossi, solidi et oboli pariter cudantur.

De admixtione vero quanta esse debeat: an grossi et solidi fiant, an etiam denarii argentei qui fertonem vel marcham mediam aut etiam integram valeant, in placito est eorum quorum interest; nisi ut modus sit et ita decernatur, ut in futurum perpetuo maneat.

De obolis quoque ratio habenda est, quomodo omnino parum nunc valent, ita ut integra marcha vix supra unius grossi argentum contineat.

Postrema autem difficultas oritur ex contractibus et obligationibus ante et post innovationem monete factis. In quibus modum invenire oportet ne contrahentes nimium graventur. Quemadmodum pristinis temporibus factum est, ut patet ex his que in altero latere hujus folii descripta sunt.

Notes

1. This distinction appears to be one of Copernicus's most serious points, as will be seen in its applications later. The French translation by Wolowski 1864 and the German translation by Sommerfeld 1978, as well as the four previous English translations by Taylor 1955, Moore 1965, Reiss 1979, and Rosen 1985 have been helpful for clarifying many choices in my translation.

2. The Latin word *aes* refers usually to an alloy of mostly copper and a small amount of tin, known as bronze (not brass). This alloy is in turn alloyed with silver in the making of silver coins.

3. Later in the essay it is explained that 1/15th of the silver value was allowed for this — at least in the early days.

4. That is, in ingot, bar, or bullion form.

5. This can happen when money is circulating with the same "face value" but quite different material values: if you can tell the difference between a silver-rich coin and a silver-poor coin, it would make sense to smelt the good ones down and produce a greater quantity of the cheaper type. This would be an instance of "Gresham's Law."

6. We should note the important difference between the metallic value of the coin being "slightly less" (Latin *paulo minus* — two paragraphs above) and "significantly less" (Latin *notabili quantitate minus*) than its power to purchase gold or silver. The former is a sign of healthy money, the latter of unhealthy.

7. Grand Master of the Teutonic Knights, 1393–1407.

8. Also known as the Battle of Grunwald. The Knights, defeated by Poles and Lithuanians, afterwards began to decline.

9. This would be 140 solids. A scot was 1/24th of a mark, and so 8 scots = ⅓ mark. Therefore, 2⅓ marks (2 marks, plus 8 scots) could in those days buy a ½-pound of pure silver. This sum would also be 140 *solidi*, or "solids" (1 mark = 60 solids; 2 x 60 = 120; 120 + 20 solids [i.e., ⅓ of 60, which is also the equivalent of 8 scots] = 140 solids).

10. The figure 112 is arrived at as follows: we now have (in our alloy) only ¾ of the original ½-pound of silver (which cost 140 solidi). That means the worth of the silver in this smaller quantity is now only 105 *solidi*. Seven *solidi* (or 1/15th of 105) are then added to this to reflect the cost of the minting itself (the bronze, the stamping, etc.): 105 + 7 = 112.

11. Copernicus appears now to be showing the consistency of the old system by explaining how the outcome coin value of the ¾-silver–¼-copper alloy can be computed a different way: by starting with the original ½-pound of silver — to which the 1/4th part of bronze has already been alloyed (i.e., already a full 140 solids' worth of silver) — we would still have to *add* something to reflect the value of the minting, as before. Again, the proportion of the small addition would be the same (i.e., 9⅓ solids' worth, or exactly 1/15th of 140), for a total of 149⅓ solids.

12. These reigns cover the years 1352–1410 (see Reiss and Hinderliter 1979, p.307, n. 54, and Sommerfeld 1978, p. 79).

13. Heinrich Reuss reigned 1410–13.

14. This point illustrates how the "½-pound weight" (or "weight mark") used for making 112 solidi was always a ½-pound of *alloyed* metal, but now with the proportion of pure silver ever shrinking, it is ¼ silver, ¾ copper.

15. See Reiss and Hinderliter 1979, p. 307 n. 56, who correct the names. The period is 1413–40.

16. In the second half of the fifteenth century, a large part of Prussia became subject to the Polish crown ("Royal Prussia"). The eastern parts were still under the Teutonic knights until 1525, when they became a secular dukedom in feudal subordination to the Kingdom of Poland ("Ducal Prussia"). The area where Copernicus lived (Varmia) was yet-another semi-independent ecclesiastical province of Poland, surrounded on three sides by Ducal Prussia.

17. The steps of the decline would be (a) ¾ silver–1/4th copper: about 5 marks per pound of silver; (b) 3/5th silver–2/5th copper: about 6 marks and 10 solidi for a pound of silver; (c) 1/4th silver–3/4th copper: about 16 marks per pound of silver; (d) reform under Michael and Rusdorff: ½ silver–½ copper: 8 marks per pound of silver ("new shillings"); (e) new coinages of the cities: 1/5th silver– 4/5th copper: 20 marks per pound of silver.

18. We should recall from an earlier paragraph that the *scot* was worth 1/24th of a mark. Now, setting 8 marks' worth of *new schillings* (60 x 8 = 480 schillings to a pound of silver) beside 20 marks of the "recent" schillings (60 x 20 = 1,200 schillings to a pound of silver), shows that the new were exactly 2 ½ times as valuable as the old (8 x 2.5 = 20). Since 24 x 2.5 = 60, it was reasonable to redefine a new schilling as a scot (or 1/24th) of the light (or cheap) mark.

19. Copernicus seems to be referring here to the change from the 16-mark pound (= stage c in n. 17 above) to the 20-mark pound (= stage e), since an inflation of 4 marks is exactly 1/5th of 20.

20. Reiss and Hinderliter 1979, p. 308. The use of multiple coinages from the variety of neighboring states is clearly another part of the problem.

21. This is the narration promised earlier: how *solidi* became *grossi*.

22. There are now 20 groats to the mark in the place of 60 schillings: 3 (old) schillings now make 1 groat (instead of 2 ½ old schillings being the equivalent of the new schilling-turned-scot). An inflation from 2 ½ to 3 is "a fifth or sixth part" (1/5th of 2 ½ and 1/6th of 3).

23. A touch of humor. New schillings became scots (and disappeared), but then groats got revenge by "taking over" the old schillings, 3 to 1.

24. Taylor 1955 has it thus: "[the] habit of melting down money and re-issuing it at a debased value"; Reiss 1979 has it as the "custom ... of counterfeiting, clipping and altering money." Taylor's rendition seems closer to the meaning in the context, where the quasi-official actions of local minting enterprises is in question, rather than sheer criminal "counterfeiting."

25. The sentences in italics appear in three manuscripts but were crossed out in two. Since the sentences recommend only a single mint for both Prussias, the attempt to remove the passage probably reflects the interests of Ducal Prussia in having its own mint rather than sharing a single mint with

other parts of Prussia. If the sentences in italics are omitted, the treatise tactfully leaves aside the disagreement between the king and the duke on this point.

26. Duke Albrecht (1490–1568), the former grand master of the Teutonic Knights, ruled his part of Prussia after April 8, 1525, as a secular (and Lutheran) fief of the Kingdom of Poland. Since the word *duke* (Latin *dux, ducis*) is used here instead of *Magister* as with earlier rulers, the document has been dated to after April 8, 1525, and probably before July 17, 1526, when a royal decree concerning new currency brought some, but not all, of Copernicus's recommendations into effect. See Rosen 1985, p. 171.

27. This appears to refer to the new regulations that would be put into effect on July 17, 1526.

28. Note again Copernicus's emphasis on the delicate balance between too much and too little metallic worth: if the money is too "rich" in silver, it will be tempting to re-melt it down at some later time; if it is too "lean" in silver, the mint authorities will be making a profit on debased coinage.

29. There is a divergence among the previous English translators at this point in the text. Rosen's interpretation seems to be the most correct one, but I have followed the Latin wording somewhat more closely: I have translated "summam … nimium multiplicatam" as "total … excessively increased" (as opposed to Rosen's "aggregate's … quantity excessive" (Rosen 1992, p. 193). This would describe "Gresham's Law."

30. That is, in ingot, bar, or bullion.

31. This would explain why 110 instead of 100 florins is used as the basis for counting.

32.That is, 1 lb. silver = 20 marks; 11 lbs. silver = 220 marks; and thereby 2 marks = 1 florin, because 110 florins = 1 lb. gold.

33. I follow Rosen 1992, p. 212 n. 80, and not Sommerfeld 1978 in reading *VIIII* (as in one of the mss.) instead of *VIII*. There are 60 solidi per mark; 20 marks = 1,200 solidi or schillings, and if this buys 12/11th of a pound of silver, then 1/11th of that would be = 100 schillings; ½ of one pound of silver would be 5.5/11, or 550 schillings; and 550 schillings = 540 schillings + 10 schillings, and 540 schillings equals *nine*, not *eight*, times sixty. (To use Copernicus's terminology, the *valor* would be 1,100 schillings, but the *aestimatio* 1,200).

34. Note the ironic touch to this ("Plan B") recommendation.

35. As Rosen 1992, p. 212 n. 80, explains, this would devalue the Prussian mark by 1/3.

36. See Rosen, 1985 for a translation of the (highly detailed and circumstantial) list omitted here. For reasons of space and relevance, it has been omitted here.

37. The text is that of L. Wolowski, (Paris, 1864).

ABOUT THE AUTHOR

NICOLAUS COPERNICUS (1473–1543) was a Renaissance polymath who made one of history's most significant astronomical contributions: he formulated a model of the universe that placed the Sun rather than the Earth at its center. A lifelong resident of Royal Prussia, he was a true multi-discipline scholar: an astronomer, mathematician, physician, classics scholar, diplomat, and economist.

The publication of this heliocentric model in his book *De revolutionibus orbium coelestium* (On the Revolutions of the Celestial Spheres) in 1543 triggered the Copernican Revolution and was a pioneering event of the Scientific Revolution.

Made in the USA
Monee, IL
04 November 2026

67377184R00056